CRIMINAL LAW FOR NON-CRIMINALS

100 Most Misunderstood Legal Principles, Clarified

Professor Giles
Wayne Casaleggio

Copyright © 2021 Professor Giles Wayne Casaleggio

All rights reserved

No part of this book may be reproduced, or stored in a retrieval system, or transmitted in any form or by any means, electronic, mechanical, photocopying, recording, or otherwise, without express written permission of the publisher.

ISBN: 9798716437319

Edited by: Chris Casaleggio

CONTENTS

Title Page	
Copyright	
To the Reader	
Introduction	1
Part One: Quizzes	9
American Legal History Quiz	10
Constitutional Law Quiz	13
Legal System Quiz	16
Criminal Procedure Quiz	19
Search and Seizure Quiz	22
Law of Evidence Quiz	25
Penal Law Quiz	28
Corrections Quiz	31
Criminology Quiz	34
Enforcing Drug Laws Quiz	37
Part Two: Answers	41
Answers to the American Legal History Quiz	42
Answers to the Constitutional Law Quiz	47
Answers to the Legal System Quiz	52

Answers to the Criminal Procedure Quiz	57
Answers to the Search and Seizure Quiz	64
Answers to the Law of Evidence Quiz	68
Answers to the Penal Law Quiz	73
Answers to the Corrections Quiz	77
Answers to the Criminology Quiz	80
Answers to the Enforcing Drug Laws Quiz	84
Epilogue	87
Appendix	89
About The Author	93
Books By This Author	95

TO THE READER

Criminals generally become legal experts in one of two ways. Initially, they learn criminal law and procedure through the experience of being dragged through the various stages of the justice system from arraignment, motions, hearings, trials, sentencings, and appeals. Laypeople generally only experience limited access to in-person criminal court activities through jury duty service. Additionally, however, criminals also study law intensely while being incarcerated. Prison law libraries and law courses are very popular, as many inmates become involved in assisting in the preparation of their own appeals. Obviously, their interest in law is intense and more than just a casual hobby.

Everyone is presumed to know the law. Ignorance of the law is no excuse. Everyone is familiar with these legal clichés, but are they accurate? Aside from some attorneys, criminals are the most familiar with the criminal laws and procedures. Laypeople generally only recognize how criminal justice is depicted on television and in movies. Unfortunately, these depictions are most often inaccurate due to the fact that it is necessary to glamorize and scandalize the events to maintain the interest of viewers. When confronting students enrolled in their first law course, it is shocking to discover the myths that they harbor concerning the basic principles of our legal system.

INTRODUCTION

My experience in the law started when I was in college, originally attempting to obtain a degree in electrical engineering. I found my mathematics courses very rewarding since I was able to successfully solve problems by defining a single, precise, correct answer to each math exam question. After changing my major to business administration, I was forced to take three credits in a law course. That course totally shook the foundation of my ideas about problem-solving.

Contrary to my previous beliefs, I learned that:

In law, there are no single, precise answers to anything.

The things that I was confident that I knew about the law were probably incorrect.

A jury never finds a defendant innocent.

A house can never be robbed.

In court, the truth is not that important.

The primary purpose of the justice system is not to dispense justice.

The goal of the prosecution is not the conviction of the offender.

This was the opposite of everything that I had learned in my educational life to that point. So how does a law professor approach the teaching of this unorthodox subject matter?

A fictitious television character named George Costanza discovered that since everything that he did ended poorly, then doing the opposite of his instincts must be the correct manner to reach success. George then began to act opposite to his instincts and was romantically and professionally successful. I believe that there may be some merit to this concept in studying law. In law school, I sometimes brought my exams home and asked my father to guess at the answers. Since he had been trained as a plumber and pipefitter, I was shocked to see how accurate his answers proved.

I now believe that before teaching legal principles, it may be preferable to un-teach many of the things that have already been learned about law since so many of the common clichés are inaccurate. In addition, I find that methods of studying law are quite dissimilar from those of other disciplines.

Instead of grading law students on whether or not they have deciphered the correct answer, they should be graded upon the reasoning in arriving at any answer.

In other words, in order to rearrange a law student's manner of thinking to conform to the way lawyers think, it may be preferable to attempt the opposite of the way in which students learned in the past.

It may be necessary to first instruct students to reject many of the things that they had previously learned about United States history. In effect, it might be a reasonable option to teach students to unlearn many of the principles which they have accepted throughout their educational lives. Beginning in 1995, James Loewen wrote books, including *Lies Across America*, which addressed the mistruths spread through inaccurate historical markers and educational curricula in the United States, which he called "Eurocentric." My belief, however, is that these myths were essentially taught because they were uncomplicated and easy to understand, they sounded logical, they expressed patriotism, and were generally pleasurable concepts.

These principles were easily introduced into the educational examinations which teachers prepared for their students since grading involved merely identifying one specific answer which corresponded to the information in the textbook. There is one correct answer to every question, and if a student selects the proper one, a superior grade is received in the class. This makes students feel that life is uncomplicated and manageable and that there is a correct answer to everything.

Unfortunately, the study of law involves interpreting judicial opinions, statutes, legal procedures, and factual situations in dispute. There is never one correct answer, but merely different opinions expressed by judges, legislators, attorneys, and jurors. Even in a case where there is agreement upon a verdict or appeal, the participants often agree for different reasons. A legal opinion issued by a panel of judges may contain a majority decision, one or more dissenting opinions, and possibly a concurring opinion. Which is the correct answer? What is the truth?

Determining the truth has become an extremely complex activity. In acquiring knowledge of current events, there is generally only a choice between liberal media and conservative media such as CNN versus Fox News. Each side will attempt to influence opinions of an event based on the agenda of the media outlet. They will flavor the news reporting based upon their perception of the political beliefs of their consumers, ensuring the continuing patronage to their services. We cannot blindly accept the interpretations of the events that are presented by them.

As students studying law, they will not have the luxury of blindly accepting the opinionated answers of others, including their professors. Before forming an opinion concerning a legal issue, they must conduct research, verify findings, reject inconsistencies, formulate plausible alternative theories, utilize skepticism, employ creative thinking, and then test their most favorable hypothesis. In this process, no theory can be dismissed as ludicrous. Historically, royal families employed "court jesters" as entertainers to provide creative thoughts which otherwise would have been considered ridiculous, disrespectful, or heresy. This inspiration sometimes provided the solutions to serious problems. For example, only the court jester could insist that the world might not be flat, and his role as a comedian protected him from prosecution. In modern times, it has been suggested that standup comedians may have the highest IQs. In legal practice, some of the most ridiculous legal defenses have been successful. The Florida trial of murderer Casey Anthony was a prime example.

In law classes, students are not tested to determine whether or not they have reached the correct answer but to determine the adequacy of reasoning skills in reaching the issue or issues presented. It may be impossible to grade a student for reaching a fruitful answer since the reasoning behind the answer might be flawed.

In American law, lawmakers, like legislators, governors, and presidents, are encouraged to express their ideas on new rules that they will offer for passage into law. In the third branch of government, the court system, judges may not express their ideas for new rules that will, in their opinions, help society. They must hold their opinions until a dispute arrives in the court system by way of an official proceeding such as a trial or appeal. Only then can judges invoke their ideas about a particular legal rule. It is called the "case in controversy rule." An actual factual case must exist, or no hypothetical advice can be given by judges on the law.

These cases that arrive on the court's doorstep do not usually involve earth-shattering problems. They are usually relatively trivial disputes only important to the participants of the matter. However, these cases give the courts the opportunity to speak and create rules and doctrines which will have the authority of law. Therefore, the most earth-shattering judicial opinions may be born during the litigation of the most unimportant disputes.

For example, the most important case in the history of the court system involved whether a man's paperwork to be appointed as a lower court judge was efficiently delivered. In most of these matters, there is really no factual scenario that average citizens consider important. Yet, the legal decision may have a major effect upon their lives.

Other important cases include such mundane situations as to whether a ferry boat operator could be licensed by a state to operate on the Hudson River and whether the working conditions of a hotel maid were fair. Both situations provided the opportunity for the United States Supreme Court to drastically change the history of American society.

※ ※ ※

The following categories contain statements of law and governmental history which may be misunderstood by the average American.

This exercise represents some common historical or legal facts that most Americans believe that they are firmly prepared to answer concerning the foundations of our legal system and our democratic republic.

Decide if a statement is most likely "**true or false**" and provide the reasoning which supports your answer.

PART ONE: QUIZZES

AMERICAN LEGAL HISTORY QUIZ

1. The Continental Congress approved a declaration of independence from the British on July 4th, 1776.

※ ※ ※

2. A member of a famous, patriotic American family submitted the original motion to declare independence to the Continental Congress.

※ ※ ※

3. We do not presently have a national United States holiday which marks the date that President Thomas Jefferson and President John Adams died.

※ ※ ※

4. The commanding general of our Continental Army, which defeated the British in The Revolutionary War, became our country's first president.

※ ※ ※

5. The original United States Constitution was written by Thomas Jefferson.

※ ※ ※

6. There has never been a situation where a president of the United States has ever successfully used his power to threaten the United States Supreme Court into changing its opinions.

※ ※ ※

7. There has never been a situation where a president of the United States used federal military troops against state law enforcement authorities to enforce a decision of the United States Supreme Court.

※ ※ ※

8. Despite the absence of any Constitutional rights, African-American slaves volunteered and fought as soldiers against the British invasion of the Washington DC and Baltimore areas during the war of 1812.

※ ※ ※

9. Andrew Jackson's defeat of the British in the Battle of New Orleans was instrumental in ending

the war of 1812, which led to his election as President and his refusal to follow the rulings of The Supreme Court recognizing the land rights of Native Americans.

❋ ❋ ❋

10. Although during the early history of the United States Supreme Court, many of the justices had been slaveowners, no former member of the Ku Klux Klan was ever permitted to serve on the court.

CONSTITUTIONAL LAW QUIZ

1. At the present time, all clauses which supported the practice of slavery have been eliminated from the United States Constitution.

❊ ❊ ❊

2. The United States Constitution gives the United States Supreme Court the power to judge whether federal and state laws are constitutional.

❊ ❊ ❊

3. In 1964, it was illegal for married couples to purchase condoms to control reproduction in southern states like Alabama, unlike all of the more liberal northeastern states.

❊ ❊ ❊

4. Should the Congress of the United States disagree with the interpretation given to the United States Constitution by the United States Supreme Court, the Constitution may be amended simply by obtaining a two-thirds majority in the House of

Representatives and the United States Senate.

* * *

5. A criminal prosecutor's duty is to represent the interests of the victim of the crime and attempt to convict the defendant of the most serious charges. The defense attorney and judge will be the protectors of the rights of the defendant.

* * *

6. The United States Constitution prevents a person from being tried twice for the same criminal episode.

* * *

7. After the Congress and states adopted the equality Amendments to the Constitution at the end of the Civil War, the United States Supreme Court has never issued rulings which deny a person the opportunity to become a naturalized citizen or own land solely because of their race or physical appearance.

* * *

8. Article III of The Constitution is the most detailed and comprehensive article since it defines the

organization and jurisdiction of the federal court system.

* * *

9. After his appeal in Miranda vs. Arizona, the family of defendant Ernesto Miranda was thankful for the Supreme Court ruling requiring the police to warn suspects of their Constitutional Rights prior to custodial interrogation.

* * *

10. When the first 10 amendments, known as the Bill of Rights, were added to the Constitution, the First Amendment created the rights of free speech and exercise of religion.

LEGAL SYSTEM QUIZ

1. The criminal court system's main purpose is to uncover the factual truth of criminal allegations.

❈ ❈ ❈

2. Upon discovering a break-in and theft occurring while a family was on vacation, a citizen is correct in calling 911 to tell the police that the house was robbed.

❈ ❈ ❈

3. When a jury's verdict finds a criminal defendant innocent on all charges, the judge must set the defendant free.

❈ ❈ ❈

4. A competent criminal defense attorney will initially ask a prospective client whether or not he actually committed the offense.

❈ ❈ ❈

5. Circumstantial evidence is weak and inadequate for convicting an offender.

* * *

6. An offender convicted in the juvenile court of a heinous act of violence will receive a criminal record which may exclude him from many civil liberties in the future.

* * *

7. In order to become a judge, it will first be necessary to graduate from law school and pass a bar examination.

* * *

8. The federal court system and the 50 State Court systems all operate under the concept of common law, originally adopted from the British.

* * *

9. The existence of the Constitution as the nation's supreme legal document is unable to be challenged with any legal criticism.

❊ ❊ ❊

10. Evidence which reveals the absolute truth of a criminal allegation is always allowed to be admitted in a trial.

CRIMINAL PROCEDURE QUIZ

1. A successful appeal cannot be obtained by alleging that the defendant's trial counsel was not competent in trial tactics.

❋ ❋ ❋

2. After a defendant is convicted of a capital offense by a jury, the judge may sentence him to execution in states having the death penalty.

❋ ❋ ❋

3. A court will never accept a guilty plea from a person continuing to express his innocence of the offense.

❋ ❋ ❋

4. A criminal court can never incarcerate an offender, finding him violent and dangerous to the public, prior to a determination of the criminal charges at his trial or by his plea bargain.

❋ ❋ ❋

5. If a criminal asks an undercover agent whether or not he is a police officer and the undercover agent lies about his law enforcement status, any related charges will be dismissed because of the doctrine of entrapment.

❋ ❋ ❋

6. The information given to patrol officers by the police dispatcher concerning a reported crime is hearsay and not admissible in court at a trial.

❋ ❋ ❋

7. It is illegal for police to use trickery or deception to entice a defendant to confess to a crime. The confession would be inadmissible in court.

❋ ❋ ❋

8. During jury selection, a trial attorney must always express a valid reason why he or she is excluding a juror from sitting on the case.

❋ ❋ ❋

9. If a defendant in a criminal case does not wish to take the witness stand and testify, the prosecutor can argue that he is concealing evidence of his guilt.

�֍ ✤ ✤

10. On a traffic stop, a driver's rights are violated if police hold him until a canine unit can be called to the scene in order to utilize an evidence detection dog to sniff his automobile exterior without his consent or a warrant.

SEARCH AND SEIZURE QUIZ

1. Police may not search a person's yard or garbage for evidence of a crime without consent or a warrant.

❊ ❊ ❊

2. Investigative stops and frisks without probable cause of a crime are illegal and violate constitutional law.

❊ ❊ ❊

3. If the police find evidence through the use of a search warrant, the prosecution has the burden of proving, prior to trial at a motion to suppress the evidence, that the search was legal.

❊ ❊ ❊

4. If police have a search warrant for illegal drugs and they find child pornography, they may not legally seize it as evidence of a crime.

❊ ❊ ❊

5. If an offender commits a burglary in New York and is found a day later in New Jersey, he can be arrested and immediately returned to the state of New York.

* * *

6. The day after a victim has been mugged, the police may show the victim a photograph assuring the victim that they have adequate evidence that this photograph was of the guilty party.

* * *

7. If a private security guard illegally searches a person and finds contraband, the criminal court will suppress the evidence.

* * *

8. A telephone service provider may secretly overhear conversations of its customers, but if a criminal conversation is overheard, they may not alert law enforcement to begin a court-ordered wiretap.

* * *

9. In order to investigate a crime, there is no legal method allowing law enforcement officers to

secretly break into a person's home in order to plant an electronic eavesdropping device to secure evidence and later secretly break into the home again to retrieve the device.

※ ※ ※

10. Generally, recording conversations secretly without judicial authority is legally permissible only if that the party recording is speaking in the conversations.

LAW OF EVIDENCE QUIZ

1. If a dying man reveals the person who shot him to a police officer, the officer can testify in court to the statement of the dying man due to the statement not being considered legal hearsay.

❈ ❈ ❈

2. Illegal confessions obtained by police without Miranda warnings can never be used in a criminal trial.

❈ ❈ ❈

3. A lawyer may not reveal to police confidential information received from a client about his planning to commit a financial crime to raise bail money.

❈ ❈ ❈

4. In a murder trial, only the actual weapon alleged to be used to cause the death may be shown to the jury in order for them to visualize the appearance and function of the murder weapon.

❈ ❈ ❈

5. In the trial of a violent offense, gruesome crime scene photographs are always admissible as evidence against the offender.

* * *

6. A wife may not testify in criminal court against her husband, who she witnessed abusing their children while they were married.

* * *

7. A witness testifying in court may not use someone else's writing in order to help him remember the relevant facts surrounding the criminal episode.

* * *

8. A photograph will only be admitted in court if the photographer takes the stand and authenticates it. Similarly, only the person who writes a business record may testify to its authenticity for it to be admissible in a trial.

* * *

9. It is objectionable for a leading question to be asked of a witness on cross-examination by the prosecutor.

※ ※ ※

10. If a witness's testimony is not in any way related to the facts of the case, the proper objection to be raised is "irrelevant."

PENAL LAW QUIZ

1. A person who initiates an adversarial conflict and is then is assaulted and injured may legally retaliate against his attacker.

❊ ❊ ❊

2. Common law developed in England originally from the statutes passed by the British Parliament.

❊ ❊ ❊

3. The crime of burglary today is almost identical to the definition under early common-law.

❊ ❊ ❊

4. At early common-law, a felony was defined as a crime which carried a long term of imprisonment.

❊ ❊ ❊

5. Assault and battery is an offense in the criminal court rather than a civil court action.

❊ ❊ ❊

6. Landowners may not attack trespassers on their land but have no duty to protect them from danger if they post a no trespassing sign on the property.

❃ ❃ ❃

7. Since the 20th century, which led to the establishment of civil unions and the rights of same-sex couples, homosexual, consensual sexual acts in the privacy of the home have been noncriminal.

❃ ❃ ❃

8. If a woman stabs her husband 40 times in his bed while she believes that he is sleeping, she is guilty of the crime of attempted homicide, even if he had previously died of a heart attack.

❃ ❃ ❃

9. It is not possible for a person to be convicted of a crime, even if the offender had an evil intent when it is proven that he failed to take any action in furtherance of the crime.

✽ ✽ ✽

10. Rape has always been considered to be a malum prohibitum type crime which, in Latin, means conduct which is prohibited.

CORRECTIONS QUIZ

1. When the concept of incarceration of offenders in prison-type facilities began, the Roman Catholic Church protested this type of inhumane treatment.

❊ ❊ ❊

2. The fictional story written by Victor Hugo about an imprisoned French criminal (*Les Misérables*) has nothing to do with the actual history of criminal justice.

❊ ❊ ❊

3. The concept of using legal insanity as a defense to capital punishment was first argued by Clarence Darrow, defending two illiterate boys charged with murder.

❊ ❊ ❊

4. The legality of capital punishment in the United States has always been consistent with the United States Constitution's prohibition on cruel and unusual punishment.

❊ ❊ ❊

5. Jails and prisons are essentially the same type of institutions, except that prisons are able to house a greater number of inmates.

❋ ❋ ❋

6. In the United States, it is illegal for lower court judges, lacking law degrees, to try cases without juries and sentence defendants to periods of incarceration in jails.

❋ ❋ ❋

7. Probation and parole officers often obtain search warrants in order to monitor the lifestyles of their offenders in their homes without prior notice of the search.

❋ ❋ ❋

8. Reducing the numbers of old age offenders from the prison system is a major benefit to the duties of the correctional staff.

❋ ❋ ❋

9. Sexual behavior between an inmate and a corrections officer is considered a reason for suspension or dismissal as a violation of prison regulations and not a criminal offense if there was

mutual consent.

※ ※ ※

10. In the United States, all prison inmates are assured that the correctional staff where they are confined has sworn to uphold the Constitution and comply with all statutory law.

CRIMINOLOGY QUIZ

1. There has never been a legal method for a person to change his race in order to alter crime statistics.

❊ ❊ ❊

2. Seasonal climate and weather conditions have not been associated with major increases or decreases in crime statistics.

❊ ❊ ❊

3. The number of police officers employed by a city is the most important demographic statistic affecting the crime rate.

❊ ❊ ❊

4. There is not a specific, logical reason why police uniforms are generally colored blue rather than some other color.

❊ ❊ ❊

5. In the United States during the early 1900s, the most dangerous terrorist organization was controlled by African-Americans.

✽ ✽ ✽

6. In the United States during the 1860s, federal troops were sent to Alabama to stop white rioters from killing African-American children in an orphanage.

✽ ✽ ✽

7. During the 1700s, the first police detective squad was organized by a decorated police chief at Scotland Yard.

✽ ✽ ✽

8. The most important American Mafia prosecutions prior to 1900 occurred in New York and Chicago.

✽ ✽ ✽

9. In the United States, the concept of establishing federal law enforcement agencies such as the FBI and Secret Service was the idea of a Civil War general from Illinois.

✽ ✽ ✽

10. Consistent reporting methods by police

departments in the United States are generally effective in establishing valid crime rate statistics published by the Federal Bureau of Investigation.

ENFORCING DRUG LAWS QUIZ

1. During the 1960s, The Federal Bureau of Investigation was pursuing the prosecution of the American Mafia and produced the first major informant to testify against organized crime.

❉ ❉ ❉

2. In states like Colorado, where marijuana is legal for recreational use, it is impossible to be prosecuted for possessing small amounts of the substance.

❉ ❉ ❉

3. There has never been a situation where the American President supported foreign narcotics trafficking into the United States in order to further his foreign policies.

❉ ❉ ❉

4. Heroin was developed in an illicit lab to be sold as a black market, addictive drug.

❉ ❉ ❉

5. Powder cocaine is much less harmful than crack cocaine.

❋ ❋ ❋

6. Statistics show that drug laws in the United States are strictly enforced throughout all segments of the American population, despite claims by minority populations that racial profiling is being utilized.

❋ ❋ ❋

7. Fentanyl is a drug that must be intentionally or accidentally inhaled or ingested to be dangerous.

❋ ❋ ❋

8. If nothing of value is received in return, cocaine may be passed on to another person at a party without the possibility of the crime of illegal distribution being charged.

❋ ❋ ❋

9. A narcotics dealer will subject himself to the same legal penalties if he sells illegal substances in the privacy of his own home, automobile, or on a public street.

❋ ❋ ❋

10. Public School personnel must have probable cause in order to search their students, just as police would need.

PART TWO: ANSWERS

ANSWERS TO THE AMERICAN LEGAL HISTORY QUIZ

The Continental Congress approved a declaration of independence from the British upon a motion made by Richard Henry Lee on July 2, 1776. This Lee family of Virginia produced Confederate General Robert E. Lee generations later. Thomas Jefferson, who many believe authored the Declaration of Independence, was on a committee which wrote a formal declaration submitted two days later. Independence Day was originally celebrated on July 2nd but was changed years later due to the fact that President Thomas Jefferson and President John Adams both died on July 4, 1826. Independence Day was later moved to July 4th in their memory. The commanding general of our Continental Army was George Washington; however, he did not become our first national president.

In March 1781, the Articles of Confederation, a federal document which preceded the Constitution, went into effect. The Articles of Confederation stipulated that there would be elected presidents fulfilling one-year terms. Samuel Huntington had been serving as president of the Continental Congress at that time and remained until July when Samuel Johnston was elected president. Johnston declined the office, and Thomas McKean was elected, and he served only until November. John Hanson was then elected and served his full one-year term pursuant to the Articles of Confederation. During the existence of the Articles of Confederation as our national document, 10 different presidents served, and several others had served prior to the Articles being adopted. Samuel Huntington, Thomas McKean, John Hanson, Elias Boudinot, Thomas Mifflin, Richard Henry Lee, John Hancock, Nathaniel Gorham, Arthur St. Clair, and Cyrus Griffin all served. John Hanson was the first president to serve a full term under the authority of the Articles of Confederation. George Washington can only be considered our first president to be elected pursuant to the United States Constitution, which superseded the Articles of Confederation.

Thomas Jefferson did not draft the original United States Constitution. In fact, he was in France at that time and was seriously opposed to the document due to its concentration on federal powers over the powers of the states. He did, however, favor the incorporation of the first 10 amendments known as the Bill of Rights. At that time, Jefferson's political party was violently opposed to the political party of President John Adams, known as the Federalists. In fact, this political rivalry led to the fatal gun duel between Vice President Arron Burr and Alexander Hamilton.

During the War of 1812, the British attacked and burned most public buildings in Washington DC in the summer of 1814. The British then turned their attack to Baltimore but failed to defeat the American Garrison at Fort McHenry, which inspired Francis Scott Key to write a poem known as the "Star-Spangled Banner." Key never wrote the melody, which was borrowed from an old English drinking song. At the outset of these battles, the British had recruited African-American slaves as soldiers to fight against American troops. Andrew Jackson's victory at the Battle of New Orleans had not been instrumental in ending the war of 1812 due to the fact that the battle was fought 15 days after a peace treaty had been signed in Europe. Based upon this victory, he was later elected President of the United States and refused to obey a decision of the United States Supreme Court concerning the rights of Native Americans resulting in a massacre known as "The Trail of Tears." In addition, his appointment of Chief Justice Roger Taney led to the decision in Dred Scott vs. Sandford that blacks, slaves or free, could never be citizens of the United States.

The First and Second Amendments to the United States Constitution clearly refer to natural or God-given rights which already existed. The First Amendment prohibits laws which abridge the right of the people to speak or assemble or to petition for a redress of grievances. The Second Amendment states that the right of the people to keep and bear arms shall not be infringed. These amendments to the Constitution clearly do not create rights but merely acknowledge that these rights are pre-existing either from common-law or natural law.

Due to the continued rulings in favor of wealthy business entrepreneurs and against efforts to protect labor, in 1937, President Franklin Delano Roosevelt threatened the United States Supreme Court with the possibility of successfully nominating up to fifteen new justices. The court had adopted the doctrine of social Darwinism, which meant that survival of the fittest applied to business enterprises as well as the evolution of animal and plant species. Since his threat was supported by the United States Senate, the court capitulated and began to rule in favor of restrictions upon working conditions and in support of organized labor.

In 1954 in the matter of Brown vs. Board of Education of Topeka Kansas (1), the Supreme Court ruled that the previous doctrine of "separate but equal" was unconstitutional. The doctrine had been established previously in the case of Plessy vs. Ferguson (2), which found the segregation of negroes to be constitutional. In 1957, in support of the Court's ruling, President Dwight D Eisenhower sent United States military soldiers of the one hundred and first airborne to Little Rock, Arkansas, to escort nine African-American students into the high school. The governor of the state of Arkansas had unsuccessfully sent police and the state's National Guard to prevent the students from entering.

In 1937, President Franklin Delano Roosevelt appointed Hugo L. Black to the United States Supreme Court, where he served for 34 years. Black had been a lawyer in Birmingham, Alabama, and a member of the United States Senate. He explained that in order to be successful as a politician in his home state, it had been necessary for him to become a member of the Ku Klux Klan. Despite his background, he became one of the most liberal Supreme Court justices of all time. As a member of the extremely liberal "Warren Court," he led the other jurists in the direction of protecting the rights of persons accused of crimes.

ANSWERS TO THE CONSTITUTIONAL LAW QUIZ

The shortest Article of the United States Constitution, Article III, provides for the establishment of one United States Supreme Court and establishes its jurisdiction and the tenure of its justices. It makes no reference to the United States Supreme Court having the authority to judge the constitutionality of laws and leaves most other provisions to the discretion of the Congress and the President. In the case of Marbury vs. Madison (3), the United States Supreme Court awarded itself the authority to judge the constitutionality of laws. Although they may establish as many Supreme Court justices as they wish and as many inferior courts, neither the Congress nor the President may amend the United States Constitution. An amendment requires a two-thirds majority of Congress and a three-quarter majority of state legislatures.

The United States Constitution today still retains clauses which were designed to support the practice of slavery. Article I section 2 paragraph three discusses the apportionment of taxes based on numbers of persons differentiating those free persons from those bound to service, Indians, and other persons designated as 3/5 of a person. Slaves are counted as 3/5 of a person. Article IV section 2 paragraph three discusses persons held to service or labor within a state. In cases where such a person has escaped into another state, he shall not be discharged from such service or labor but shall be delivered up upon a claim of the party to whom service or labor may be due. This clause is obviously designed to authorize the return of runaway slaves.

Up until 1965, the state of Connecticut prohibited everyone, including married couples, from purchasing contraceptives. During that year, The United States Supreme Court, in the case of Griswold vs. Connecticut (4), found that this prohibition was unconstitutional due to a "right of privacy." This same right led to their opinion in Roe vs. Wade in 1973 (5), which legalized abortion.

In 1922 in the case of Ozawa vs. the United States (6), the United States Supreme Court ruled that a person of the Asian race could not be naturalized as a citizen of the United States. The court based its decision upon scientific studies concerning the four separate races existing in the world. In its opinion, the court stressed the concept that the United States was inhabited by people of the "white" race. In the following case that same year, the United States vs. Singh Thind, (7) the court rejected scientific evidence that persons born in India were Caucasian, explaining that Indians were not commonly recognized as "white."

Ernesto Miranda was a convicted rapist and kidnapper who appealed his conviction to the United States Supreme Court, alleging that he was compelled to confess to his crimes. The court formulated a doctrine known as the "Miranda Rule"(8), which required police to recite the constitutional rights of a person in custodial detention prior to interrogating him. In 1976 Ernesto Miranda was free and attempting to supplement his income by selling autographed Miranda warning cards. On one particular day, a dispute in a tavern found an attacker stabbing Ernesto to death. In attempting to secure a confession from the attacker, the police were required to first read him his Miranda rights. After understanding his right to remain silent, the attacker refused to speak, and police were unable to secure sufficient evidence to sustain a criminal charge.

Today's prosecuting attorneys may be described as possessing five separate identities: a licensed attorney at law, a political official, a government administrator, an investigator of crimes, and the chief law enforcement officer of his jurisdiction. Although the prosecutor's job description is complex, his duty to the public is straightforward. It is not to seek convictions or to just represent the interest of crime victims or to support the police; it is merely to seek justice. Black's Law

Dictionary describes "Justice" as the "constant and perpetual disposition to render every man his due." A distinguished Chief Justice and former state governor described the duties of the prosecutor as follows: "the power of the prosecutor sets the standard for moral leadership in the field of law enforcement. The people do not expect their minister of justice to be a witch hunter or to pour out the resources of his effort by investigating grammar school picnics to learn whether someone is selling chances on a chocolate cake. A prosecutor is bound to a higher duty than the advocacy of his cause. He is a symbol of justice. He is committed to a professionalism which would bind him, for instance, to a disclosure of facts in the very midst of the trial of his case which might very well bring about its collapse, all in the interest of justice."

The Fifth Amendment of the United States Constitution prohibits a second prosecution for the same offense by the same sovereign. It is a prohibition originally found in common-law. Sovereignty is defined as the absolute and supreme right, authority, and power under which an independent state or nation is governed. The term infers unabridged police power within its borders. In the United States, a particular act may be an offense under state law and simultaneously under federal law. In this case, the doctrine of separate sovereignty applies, and an offender may be tried in the state where the act occurred and by the federal authorities as well. A well-publicized example was the assault upon a black individual named Rodney King in California. The police officers charged with the assault were tried and acquitted by a California state jury. However, thereafter federal prosecutors charged the officers (9) with the federal violation of King's civil rights for the same incident, and they were convicted. Obviously, it is possible for an offender to be tried twice for the same act in the United States.

ANSWERS TO THE LEGAL SYSTEM QUIZ

The purpose of the criminal justice system is to resolve disputes between parties and discourage retribution and public disorder. Faith in the legitimacy of the court system is seen as a method of keeping the varied interests of the population under control. The rights of the accused, plea-bargaining, mediation, and arbitration provide incentives to negotiate and participate in a respectful adversarial contest. In fact, the rules of evidence intentionally prevent the absolute truth from being admitted in court. Examples include suppression of confessions, items seized during searches, prior criminal records, gory photographs, and the testimony of witnesses where conversations are considered privileged. The truth will be barred in situations where it tends to prejudice the jury, consume too much court time, or violate certain social values.

Robbery has, since Common Law, been a crime against a person rather than a property crime such as burglary. Although property may be stolen, it is the violence of the encounter that is the focus of the offense. For robbery to take place, a human victim must be present.

Trial juries have three alternatives. They may

unanimously find a defendant guilty, not guilty, or fail to reach a unanimous verdict resulting in a mistrial. In our system, although the defendant is presumed innocent prior to and during trial, a verdict of not guilty is not equivalent to a finding of innocence. An acquittal is only a statement by the jury to the effect that the evidence did not meet the threshold of beyond a reasonable doubt. They could have, in fact, believed in the offender's guilt but felt compelled to release him in order to criticize the law, the prosecutor, or grant the defendant mercy despite his guilt. One of the most famous trial lawyers in history, Clarence Darrow, stated that a jury will never convict a defendant that it likes, nor ever acquit a defendant that it hates. In reality, jury nullification actually exists in our system, whereby jurors may base their verdict upon considerations other than the evidence. Many have felt that the criminal court verdict in the O.J. Simpson murder trial (10) was such an example.

Being aware of the defendant's admissions of culpability in a crime poses a problem for an ethical defense attorney. It will now be impossible for the defense counsel to call the defendant to the witness stand in a trial without him implicating himself in the crime. If the defendant testifies, he must be consistent with the statement made to his attorney. If he testifies differently, his attorney will be subject to disciplinary action for permitting possible perjury to take place. For this reason, competent defense attorneys rarely ask their clients whether or not they have, in fact, committed the offense. Once the defendant begins to relate his culpability, the defense attorney is limited in constructing a defense.

The media generally refers to circumstantial evidence as weak and insufficient to successfully prosecute an offender. In reality, circumstantial evidence and direct evidence may have an equal value depending upon the facts of the case. The difference between direct and circumstantial evidence is often explained in the following scenario. If a mother walks into her kitchen and observes her child eating jam, direct evidence has been obtained since the mother is a witness who may testify to her observation. If, however, the mother enters the kitchen after the activity has ended but observes an open jam jar, her child with jam smeared over his face, a chair pulled up to a cabinet that contained the jam jar, and the cabinet door opened, she may infer circumstantially that her child had been eating the jam. The only difference between direct and circumstantial evidence is that circumstantial evidence requires an inference to be made. Many forms of scientific evidence are circumstantial, such as DNA analysis.

The rules of evidence make no general provisions for admitting all truthful testimony and physical evidence in the courtroom. Many truthful forms of evidence, for various reasons, are inadmissible.

For example, a priest's testimony is inadmissible concerning a parishioner's confession to a crime since admitting that evidence would weaken religious practices.

Juveniles who are tried in the juvenile court are always subjected to being convicted of juvenile delinquency rather than a crime. These juveniles receive no criminal record even in very serious charges such as homicide. Records of their convictions of juvenile delinquency are not public record and would only be utilized if the juvenile later reaches adulthood and commits an adult criminal offense. In this situation, a sentencing judge would be permitted to view the juvenile delinquency record to determine the sentence to impose on the adult offender. A juvenile's privacy is generally protected in the criminal court system, with the possible exception of a juvenile being referred to the adult court in an extraordinary situation where extreme violence and maturity are present.

In many states, including New York, lower court judges are elected and qualified as being adult residents of their jurisdictions. No law degree or bar admission is required, and a minimal training course is sometimes mandated. Although currently, all justices of the United States Supreme Court are attorneys admitted to the bar, there is no such requirement under law. In the United States, there are 51 Separate Court systems, as the federal system is separate and distinct from the states. Only one state, Louisiana, recognizes a system other than British common law. Due to the heritage of its original inhabitants, Louisiana recognizes French civil law, which is based upon the statutory system in France. However, this is more prevalent in its civil courts.

Although the United States Constitution is universally considered to be the foundation of all American law, it has not gone without criticism. The delegates to the Constitutional Convention in Philadelphia who adopted the Constitution had been only given authority to amend another document called the Articles of Confederation. The Articles of Confederation had preceded the Constitution as our national document but proved unworkable due to the emphasis upon the power of individual states. It may be argued that the delegates lacked authority to repeal the Articles of Confederation and then create an entirely new document titled the Constitution.

ANSWERS TO THE CRIMINAL PROCEDURE QUIZ

In order to successfully appeal a verdict and/or sentencing in the criminal court, it is necessary to show that something interfered with the fairness of the disposition of the case. Merely arguing that the jury's verdict was incorrect is inadequate since the appellate court will rely upon the transcript of the trial court's process in order to determine the fairness of its procedures. Generally, no additional evidence will be received and considered. Therefore, it is important to identify legal issues which may have interfered with the defendant's right to a fair trial. Such issues might include misconduct by the prosecutor, an incorrect instruction to the jury by the judge, the failure to alert the defense counsel of significant witnesses or articles of evidence, and the failure of defense counsel to competently conduct all of the activities relating to the defense of the accused. Many defendants have historically alleged attorney incompetence in their appeals despite the impressive credentials of their counsel.

In capital cases today, trials are separated into two phases as required by rulings of the United States Supreme Court on the Constitution's ban on cruel and unusual punishment. (11) After the verdict, a second phase of the trial, called the penalty phase, begins whereby the prosecution and defense present evidence related to the aggravating and mitigating factors relating to the defendant's personal life and his criminal acts. Generally, if the jury is unable to agree upon a verdict of the death penalty, a life sentence will be imposed. Judges alone no longer have the discretion to impose the death penalty.

Offenders lacking the financial ability to post bail often serve lengthy terms in jail facilities awaiting a disposition of their criminal cases. Since it may take years in order to complete trials of criminal cases due to volumes of backlogs, plea-bargaining has become a popular remedy in order to avoid lengthy pretrial incarceration. An offender who believes that he has been erroneously prosecuted has a choice of waiting incarcerated for a lengthy period of time or dishonestly admitting to the crime in order to secure a speedy disposition of the charges. The United States Supreme Court has ruled in the case of such a defendant that courts may accept such plea bargain agreements resulting in convictions and sentencings. (12) The ruling gives such offenders the right to negotiate plea bargains while still contending innocence, thus allowing an earlier departure from incarceration.

Generally, the determination by a criminal court on the necessity for an amount of bail is guided by the likelihood that the defendant will appear at all events scheduled in the criminal prosecution. Should facts determine that there is a high likelihood that the defendant will flee the jurisdiction rather than appearing, he may be held on a high bail or incarcerated without bail. In cases where violence is alleged, the United States Supreme Court has ruled that a pretrial determination may be made in order to determine whether or not the defendant is a threat to public safety. In a matter involving a member of organized crime, the Supreme Court established the precedent that such a finding could be made prior to the trial jury's verdict upon the allegations of violence. (13)

The legal doctrine of entrapment may be used as a defense to criminal charges. The defense requires that an offender was not predisposed to commit the crime except for the influence of law enforcement. In many criminal investigations, including organized crime and narcotics distribution, police authorities are required to utilize confidential informants and undercover police agents. Frequently, the targets of such investigations inquire about the status of persons surrounding their criminal activities. They believe that if they ask whether or not a person is an agent of law enforcement that the agent must answer truthfully, or the defense of entrapment arises. Obviously, if this was true, undercover investigations would be impossible. The United States Supreme Court has even ruled that using an undercover agent in a jail cell with an offender is a legal investigative tactic. (14)

In situations where defendants argue that their Fourth Amendment rights have been violated by police through the use of narcotics detection dogs, the United States Supreme Court has affirmed the use of such procedures on public streets and roadways as constitutional. Police may, without probable cause or reasonable suspicion, bring drug detection canines to areas surrounding persons that they wish to screen for illegal substances. (15)

Although coerced and custodial interrogations without advising an offender of Miranda rights are subject to being suppressed by criminal courts, enticing a defendant to confess to a crime is not impossible. In situations where a defendant is not in custody or where a defendant is in custody, but no interrogation is taking place, inculpatory statements by defendants are admissible in court. Police investigators are free to express falsehoods or lies in the hopes of eliciting responses from arrestees. Even in a custodial situation, as long as the conversation between investigators is not directed toward a suspect, it may elicit inculpatory responses, which will be admissible. Frequently, police falsely indicate in the presence of detainees that they have received positive DNA evidence implicating them in the crime. The courts have generally ruled in favor of this practice.

Laypeople generally realize that there is a rule of

evidence that prevents hearsay evidence from being admitted in a trial. It is believed that the definition of hearsay is a statement which has been related to a person in the form of gossip rather than personal experience. The legal definition of hearsay is much more complex. Hearsay is defined as an out-of-court statement made by a speaker other than the in-court sworn witness, offered in evidence to prove the truth of the matter asserted. This statement may be oral, a writing, or a nonverbal action. In a situation where a police dispatcher relates information received from a crime victim over the telephone to responding police patrol officers, hearsay issues may not result. At a later trial, where the patrol officers are sworn and testify, they may relate the information relayed to them by the dispatcher to explain why they arrived at the crime scene. The statement does not qualify as hearsay since it is not intended to prove the truth of a matter being litigated but merely to explain the reason why police arrived at the location of the crime.

In selecting juries for criminal cases, prosecutors and defense attorneys are permitted to interrogate prospective jurors concerning their eligibility to participate in a trial. In addition to answers to questioning, lawyers know general information about them, such as their appearance, names, employment, and the location of their residences. Each attorney is permitted to request that the judge excuse a prospective juror for what is called "cause," meaning that there is some reason why the individual may not be capable of reaching a fair verdict. In cases where attorneys are not aware of any legitimate "cause," but they believe that the juror would be unfavorable to their case presentation, they may exercise what is called a "preemptory challenge." Each lawyer is allotted a specific number of such challenges to be used, except in cases where some form of racial, religious, gender prejudice is the source of the challenge. (16) In exercising the preemptory challenge, lawyers need not verbalize any reason for their excusing an individual from the jury.

In a criminal trial, the burden of proof is put upon the prosecutor. Should the prosecutor not meet this burden, the case may be dismissed at the outset of the proceedings. In the case of defense counsel, there is no such equivalent burden of proof except in the case of the introduction of certain affirmative defenses such as insanity. Therefore, in most cases, the defense has no affirmative burden to produce any evidence and may merely proceed by attacking the evidence of the prosecutor. Most criminal defense attorneys have a difficult time in securing legitimate witnesses in order to present a defense. Defendants almost always decline to assume the witness stand and explain the circumstances of their defenses. The Fifth Amendment of the Constitution provides them with this right. Depending upon the wishes of the defendant, the judge may, or may not, explain to the jury the defendant's right to decline testifying during the trial. Should the prosecuting attorney make any comment, in the presence of the jury, concerning the failure of the defendant to testify, a mistrial will result. Even in cases where a mistrial has not been declared, on appeal, a conviction will almost always be reversed. Among the reasons for a defendant not to assume the witness stand and testify is the fact that his criminal record may become admissible in cross-examination to expose his relevant character trait, such as anger or dishonesty. In this situation, there is always a chance that the jury will interpret the prior conviction more severely than the limited use it was admitted for.

ANSWERS TO THE SEARCH AND SEIZURE QUIZ

The United States Supreme Court has ruled that garbage is abandoned property, and the owner has waived his right to protect it. (17) Additionally, the court has ruled that a privately owned open field is not subject to fourth amendment protection unless it can be considered a part of the home called its curtilage. (18) In both situations, the police are permitted to search without probable cause or warrants. If the police find evidence without the use of a search warrant, the prosecutor has the burden of proving at a proceeding prior to trial that the evidence was seized in a constitutional matter. If he fails to meet his burden by producing evidence, the defense will prevail in suppressing the evidence from use during the prosecution. When the police obtain a duly executed search warrant, the burden shifts to the defense to establish by evidence that the search was unlawful. In most cases where court-ordered search warrants are issued, searches are found to be constitutional. Under the doctrine of "plain view" (19), if police are executing a search warrant specifying that they may seize illegal narcotics and during the search they are able to observe openly child pornography, they are empowered to seize it and to use it in a prosecution of that offense. This rule only applies to readily observable contraband. Contraband is defined as any item easily observed as illegal to possess.

Under a decision of the United States Supreme Court entitled Terry v. Ohio, (20), it was held that if police, lacking "probable cause," possess a lesser standard of proof called "reasonable suspicion," they may briefly stop and hold a suspect in investigative detention to determine whether or not a crime has been committed. Also, under the standard of reasonable suspicion of weapons possession, police may pat down a suspect over the exterior of his clothing, searching for the dangerous item.

In the event that a private corporation's security guard illegally searches a person and finds contraband, the evidence found is not subject to the Constitutional "exclusionary rule," which would prevent the evidence from being used in the prosecution. Should the security guard be working in conjunction with police, the Fourth Amendment would apply. The Fourth Amendment of the Constitution, which protects a person from illegal searches, is only directed toward government officials and not private persons. Of course, the aggrieved party may always pursue litigation against the security guard for the intrusion.

In most states, when speaking in a place where other persons may overhear, the speaker takes a chance that another person is recording the conversation, and it could possibly be utilized in a court proceeding. If a person is speaking in reasonable privacy, electronic surveillance warrants would be required to record the conversation. In order to investigate a crime, police may obtain an electronic surveillance court order which would provide them with permission to secretly access the place that is being bugged. Specialized law enforcement officers are trained for this purpose by learning to defeat alarm systems and locking devices. A telephone service provider is authorized to secretly overhear conversations of its customers periodically in order to determine whether or not fraud is taking place. Should the provider determine that a criminal conversation has been overheard, the provider may notify law enforcement, and a court-ordered wiretap may be applied for by the authorities.

In cases such as robbery, police may need to have a victim identify the perpetrator of the crime. Normally, police will exhibit to the victim a number of different photographs depicting similar-looking individuals, hoping to disclose the particular perpetrator. Police are never permitted to conduct this procedure in a suggestive way. (21) If police were to show only one photograph, it is likely that the victim will believe that the police are suspicious of the person depicted. This will taint the victim's identification which will result in the identification being inadmissible in court. An exception to this rule occurs when the police arrive immediately at the crime scene and search the area for an individual fitting the victim's description. In this situation, the police may display one particular person to the victim in hopes that they have apprehended the perpetrator. This can only occur shortly after the crime has been committed. Offenders who seek to escape detection by police may flee the jurisdiction. If discovered in a neighboring state, or distant state, they may be arrested by the police of that jurisdiction and charged as being fugitives. In order for such an offender to be transported back to the state where the offense has taken place, an extradition court hearing must be held within the state where he was captured. Only then, pursuant to a judge's order, may authorities from the state where the offense occurred retrieve the suspect. There is an exception whereby police are in hot pursuit of a suspect who enters a neighboring state.

ANSWERS TO THE LAW OF EVIDENCE QUIZ

There are many hearsay statements which are defined by the rules of evidence as "exceptions" to the hearsay rule, meaning that they are admissible despite being hearsay. One such exception is labeled the "dying declaration." In a situation where a declarant is aware of his impending death, the statements that he makes about his observations will still be admissible if the party overhearing the statement later is sworn and testifies at the trial of the matter.

The United States Supreme Court has ruled that an illegally taken confession by police may be used by a prosecutor at trial on cross-examination if the defendant takes the stand and testifies inconsistently with his previous illegal confession. (22) This is an exception to the inadmissibility described by the Miranda case ruling.

Attorneys may not reveal the content of conversations with clients accused of crimes, even if they are inculpatory. Professional ethics rules prevent this from occurring with penalties, including possible disbarment. However, lawyers, as officers of the court, are required to report any information that they have received concerning their knowledge of an impending or future crime. Additionally, lawyers may not sponsor, through their witnesses, information that they are aware is false. This applies especially to the testimony of accused offenders where client interviews have previously revealed information of an inconsistent nature.

During a trial, attorneys may offer two general forms of evidence. Real evidence is such that it is directly connected to the offense being litigated. A murder weapon found at the scene of the crime, for example, would qualify as real evidence. Demonstrative evidence includes photographs, diagrams, live demonstrations, and other items which are intended to provide jurors with the ability to sort through complex matters. In situations where the actual murder weapon has not been recovered by police, prosecutors may introduce a similar weapon based upon the testimony of witnesses who have described it. Included with these forms of tangible evidence as distinguished from testimonial evidence would be crime scene photographs. In the case of the admission of gruesome, graphic, and gory crime scene photographs, a judge may fail to admit them at the trial, although they may be useful to the jury. A decision must be made as to whether the probative value of the photographs outweighs the potential prejudice to the defendant as the jury views them. If the judge believes that viewing the photographs will unfairly prejudice the jury, the photographs will be inadmissible.

It is generally known that there is a spousal privilege that limits certain types of testimony in a criminal case. For example, in most states, a wife is barred from revealing the content of confidential conversations with her husband, which revealed a criminal act by him. Generally, this privilege is not valid in situations where the wife actually witnesses a crime, or the crime has been directed at her or her children as victims.

Witnesses who testify in court are permitted to express the feeling that a particular document or other item may refresh their recollection of the incident that they are about to relate. It is not necessary that the witness be the author of the document that is being utilized. Frequently, witnesses may request a local newspaper which helps refresh the memory of a certain situation. Although the item utilized is generally not automatically submitted to the jury, it is available on the witness stand for the witness to read before stating his or her testimony. Of course, a cross-examiner may contend that the memory of the witness is flawed due to its need to be refreshed. Photographs may be admitted in evidence through sponsorship of a witness, as would any other form of real evidence. Although the photographer would certainly qualify as such a sponsor witness, it is not always necessary. Any witness with relevant knowledge of the circumstances surrounding the photograph may testify to authenticate it. For example, in the movie *My Cousin Vinny*, a local resident verified the accuracy of photographs depicting trees and bushes located at the crime scene. Similarly, any business document may be admitted in evidence through the sponsorship of the maker of the written document. However, admission is frequently accomplished through the testimony of the custodian of the business records of the organization as long as it is a document kept in the ordinary course of the business and not specially drafted for this particular prosecution.

The act of leading a witness by an attorney directing the questioning means that the question contains all of the facts to be elicited and merely calls for a yes or no answer from the witness. Unless there are special circumstances, it is objectionable for an attorney who has called a witness to use this form of questioning. However, in some situations, such as in the questioning of children, judges will allow it. In cross-examination, leading questions are not objectionable, and it is the preferred method of most well-trained trial lawyers. Leading cross-examination questions prevent witnesses from explaining their particular opinions and confine them to merely affirming or denying information. Another very common trial objection based upon the law of evidence is the objection to relevance. When a lawyer states that an objection of irrelevance should be sustained by the judge, it is meant that the testimony to be elicited from the question will not be directed toward resolving any issue to be litigated at the trial. However, if a question has no relationship at all to the matter being litigated, the proper objection would be immaterial. For example, in the trial of O.J. Simpson, a question directed toward information about a touchdown that Mr. Simpson scored in a particular football game would be immaterial to his murder charge. A question directed toward the age of his Ford Bronco might be objected to as irrelevant, since there was no issue concerning how old his automobile was at the time he may have driven it to the crime scene.

ANSWERS TO THE PENAL LAW QUIZ

Generally, a person who initiates a conflict with another person will not be able to avail himself of self-defense when he resorts to violence to fend off imminent danger of serious injury. Self-defense requires that the victim was not the aggressor, or that after being the aggressor, he clearly withdrew from the attack. Even in situations where an attack brings serious injury, retaliation may not occur after the attack has ended. A victim may not exercise preemptive attacks and then rely on self-defense to avoid legal liability. Naturally, self-defense requires that any use of force be reasonable under the circumstances and not excessive.

The defense of impossibility exists in situations where a crime may be intended but may not be accomplished due to some legal or factual incapability. For example, it is not possible to commit a homicide offense if the intended victim is already deceased. In that case, it would not even be possible to commit attempted homicide since the offender has never had the opportunity to commit the crime and then been deterred. In the crime of attempt, some occurrence prevents the offender from completing the crime. For example, a firearm jams, and the bullet never fires.

Normally, penal law requires an evil intent and a concurrent action in order to commit an offense. However, every rule in law seems to have an exception. There are crimes where nonfeasance or no action is required for an offense to be consummated. If a duty is imposed by law and there is a failure to carry out that duty, the crime has been completed. Some jurisdictions have a good Samaritan law which requires citizens to assist in some manner if they witness another person being victimized in an obvious criminal situation. A more common situation might be where a certified lifeguard fails to attempt to save a drowning swimmer.

Unfortunately, many laypeople believe that as landowners that they have the right to use violence to protect their land from unwanted trespassers. Although trespassers who illegally enter a dwelling may be treated harshly under the laws of many jurisdictions, it is clearly unlawful to use deadly force against them unless they reasonably pose a threat of serious injury or death to the homeowner. It is never lawful to use deadly force to prevent the theft of personal property. Landowners do have a reasonable duty to protect those individuals who are regarded as licensees with access to property. An example might be a postal letter carrier. Individuals who are not invitees or licensees are considered trespassers, and no duty to make them safe is imposed. However, children are the exception to this rule. Should some artificial feature of a property, such as a swimming pool, be appealing to children, it is the duty of the homeowner to protect them even though they are trespassers.

Assault and battery have been offenses since early common-law. At that time, civil and criminal cases existed interchangeably in one court. When civil law and criminal law separated, many forms of litigation existed in both systems. For example, in civil law, there is a form of action in tort, which is described as an intentional civil wrong. Tort law includes civil actions for both assault and battery as separate offenses. Assault was defined as the reasonable apprehension that an immediate battery was about to occur. Battery was defined as the unconsented touching of another. Both could result in damages being assessed. In criminal law, assault and battery have been combined into one violation. Under common law burglary, several different requirements existed in order to constitute a criminal offense. First, there had to be a (1) breaking and entering into an (2) inhabited dwelling, of (3) another nonconsenting person, (4) at night, in order to (5) commit a felony. The definition today is much more liberal.

Common Law developed from unwritten legal concepts passed down through word-of-mouth from Anglo-Saxon judge's rulings. After the Normans conquered England in 1066 A.D., these legal concepts began to be recorded by judges.

Much later, legislatures began to codify these concepts into statutes. At early common-law, a felony was defined as any crime in which the death penalty applied. At that time, most forms of theft were considered felonies. Misdemeanors subjected offenders to corporal punishment, forms of torture, and at a later time, imprisonment. At Common Law, the crime of rape was considered malum in se, being a crime of immorality. Today crimes created by modern governments such as drug possession are defined as malum prohibitum, created by government. Up until the case of Lawrence versus Texas in 2003, (23) a Supreme Court ruling allowed criminal prosecutions of homosexuals engaged in sexual relations within the privacy of their own homes. Generally, prior to 2003, if police entered the home in order to investigate suspicious activity and stumbled upon homosexual activity, they were required to make arrests, and in many southern jurisdictions, convictions were normally obtained.

ANSWERS TO THE CORRECTIONS QUIZ

The original idea of incarcerating offenders was adopted from the procedures used by the Roman Catholic Church, where cells were maintained in church basements to house sinners. Previous to incarceration, corporal punishment, execution, and assessing damages had been the punishment methods. In 1972, the United States Supreme Court ruled that practices for sentencing convicted criminals to death was unconstitutional and in violation of the Eighth Amendment of the Constitution. (24) During the 1970s, the entire process of invoking the death penalty was changed into a bifurcated trial system where the jury would have input into the level of punishment in capital cases. The concept of using legal insanity as a defense to the death penalty was successfully argued by Clarence Darrow, possibly America's greatest trial lawyer. There he was able to avoid the death penalty for two very wealthy young men who maintained genius IQ levels, claiming the insanity defense. Darrow went on to handle many other famous trials, including the Scopes Monkey Trial.

In the United States, generally, prisons house inmates who have been convicted of serious felonies. Jails, on the other hand, house inmates still awaiting trials on felony cases who are unable to make bail and offenders of misdemeanors and other lower violations which carry short incarceration sentences. Generally, they are six months or less. Still today in the United States, there are many jurisdictions where lower court judges are elected and lack any legal training. These judges are still authorized to try lower crimes without juries and sentence defendants to a maximum of six months of incarceration for each offense. Additionally, probation and parole officers may subject released offenders to certain conditions which subject them to routinely report to their offices, behave in a certain manner and allow consent to warrantless searches of their premises at any time of the day or night.

Studies have shown that the number of elderly inmates at a correctional institution is a positive factor to the benefit of the correctional staff. Older offenders tend to provide stability and guidance to younger offenders and present less of a risk of disobedience. Although it's reasonable to prioritize the release of older offenders since they are of less danger to re-offend, it is a value to have them remain within the facility to promote stability. Most jurisdictions in the United States consider consensual sexual conduct between inmates and correctional staff as felony sex crimes. This is due to the fact that where a person possesses official authority over another, consent may not be completely voluntary. Based on considerations of the economy, many jurisdictions outsource corrections functions to private corporations. In these facilities, corporate staff members are not constitutionally sworn officers and may not afford inmates the same rights and protections that government corrections officers do.

During the 1800s, Victor Hugo wrote an inspirational novel entitled *Les Misérables* about a Frenchman imprisoned for theft in Paris who escapes and leads a successful life as a businessman and mayor of his community. At the time, Hugo was aware of the life of a criminal who later became chief police inspector of Paris upon which the story is, in part, based. The individual was Eugene Françoise Vidocq, who may have also been the inspiration for the fictional stories of Sherlock Holmes. Having experience on both sides of the criminal justice system, Vidocq invented many of the modern investigation techniques utilized today.

ANSWERS TO THE CRIMINOLOGY QUIZ

Generally, the crime rate decreases in times when there is a smaller population of young men living in a particular jurisdiction. Additionally, crime rates are lower during incidents of bad weather such as blizzards. These conditions are far more definite in crime reduction than statistics representing the number of police officers per capita in a particular location. Police tend to react and respond to crime rather than attempt to prevent it. Reporting methods used by policing agencies within the United States to the Federal Bureau of Investigation are varied. They differ in crime definitions, calculating methods, whether to report the number of offenders or the number of criminal incidents or whether or not to divide incidents by the total community population. There are situations of nonreporting and errors in reporting. All of these factors make it difficult to accurately assess and compare crime rates throughout the United States. Since each state legislature has specific definitions as to the formula for attaching an individual to a particular race, such statistics may be flawed. For example, a person 75% Caucasian and 25% African-American may be considered legally black in Alabama but considered Caucasian in Virginia.

Therefore, a person may essentially change their race when traveling from one state to another.

During the 1700s, Henry Fielding, a famous British playwright who occupied the position of magistrate, organized a police squad known as the Bow Street Runners in an area of London. This was considered the first organized police detective squad. Also, in London, Robert Peel, Home Secretary of Great Britain, created the first professional paid police department. Peel wanted his officers to be servants of the people rather than occupying military soldiers. Therefore, in order to have them appear nonthreatening, he designed a long blue uniform which would hide any appearance of a weapon. Blue was the chosen color since it was distinct from the military uniform color of bright red. In the United States, the concept of federal law enforcement was begun by a Scottish barrel maker named Allan Pinkerton. Pinkerton had stumbled upon a group of counterfeiters, which he reported to authorities and was awarded a position as a deputy sheriff in Illinois. Afterward, he developed a private investigation firm which protected the railroads and banks nationwide and later saved the life of President Abraham Lincoln. From his firm, he developed the concept of the United States Secret Service as the first federal law enforcement agency of the Treasury Department. From the Treasury Department's investigation division developed the concept of the Federal Bureau of Investigation in

1926.

During the 1860s, lower Manhattan in New York City was the scene of violent civil war draft riots primarily by Irish Americans. The riots damaged property and caused the deaths of many African-Americans as well as the arson of an African-American orphanage. Troops were summoned from the battlefield of Gettysburg in order to suppress the rioting in New York City. While most laypeople and even many law enforcement officials believe that in the United States, Italian American organized crime began in New York or Chicago, it actually began in 1869 in the city of New Orleans, Louisiana. A group of Italian immigrants created a crime syndicate which they had modeled after a Sicilian crime group known as the Black Hand. The Black Hand employed the practice of sending extortion letters to Italian merchants, which bore a black handprint. In New Orleans, this scheme was primarily directed toward Italian immigrants who had memories of the brutality practiced in Sicily. In 1891 a police superintendent interceded to control a violent gang war between competing Sicilian families. He was killed execution-style. After mass arrests of Sicilians, a trial resulted in acquittals caused by tampering and intimidation of witnesses and the assistance of very clever defense attorneys. Outraged citizens of New Orleans demanded revenge directed toward the miscarriage of justice. An organized lynch mob executed 11 of the Sicilian defendants despite their acquittals.

In the early 1900s, Italian Americans, who were members of a group advocating anarchy, committed a series of armed robberies and terrorist bombings in New York and Boston. Law enforcement in the United States devoted all of its resources to the eradication of this group of dangerous terrorists. As a result, a famous case entitled "Sacco and Vanzetti" (25) was prosecuted utilizing dubious prosecution methods. Both men were convicted and executed, although many experts still see the case as an injustice.

ANSWERS TO THE ENFORCING DRUG LAWS QUIZ

During the 1960s, the director of the Federal Bureau of Investigation was denying the existence of a syndicated Italian-American organized crime problem. A minimum of FBI agents was assigned to monitor the operation of these gangsters. It was later rumored that organized crime had been blackmailing the FBI director, threatening to reveal his sexual preferences. At that time, the United States Bureau of Narcotics and Dangerous Drugs (the forerunner of the Drug Enforcement Administration) led the movement to identify the hierarchy of the American Cosa Nostra. Narcotics agents were able to turn a Mafia drug pusher, named Joseph Valachi, into an informant and exposed the network of Cosa Nostra across the United States to the United States Congress.

Narcotics distributors will subject themselves to increased legal penalties when they conduct their illegal business within their homes or automobiles as opposed to on the street. Prosecutors are able to prove in a civil proceeding, requiring much less proof than a criminal one, that a home or automobile was linked to some aspect of the illegal narcotics distribution business. The property may be seized and ownership transferred to the law enforcement agency involved. In addition, if proof shows that the money utilized to purchase the home or automobile was a result of the illegal drug distribution, the same result may occur. Of course, it is still a serious felony for an individual to pass on illegal narcotics to another even if nothing of value is exchanged. In states where recreational marijuana is permitted to be sold, possessed, and consumed, it is still possible for felony arrests to be accomplished since the federal drug law still includes marijuana as a Schedule I illegal drug.

Heroin was developed in 1898 by a German pharmaceutical company still in business worldwide. Bayer Corporation had offered it as a cough suppressant, sleep aid, and painkiller as a safer narcotic than morphine. Fentanyl is an especially dangerous narcotic for law enforcement officers to deal with since handling it exposes officers to it being transmitted by osmosis through the skin of their hands. Powder cocaine and crack are essentially the same drug and can be equally dangerous depending upon purity. The difference between these two narcotics is essentially that they are used by people of different types of income levels. Powder cocaine is more common among celebrities and wealthy individuals, while crack is more common in low-income neighborhoods. Since police are more intensely assigned to high crime areas such as ghettos where minorities reside, drug laws are more vigorously enforced there. Statistics show that harsher sentences are received in cases of illegal crack possession and distribution since prosecutions are more common in those neighborhoods. Police patrols have been described as more "service style policing" in high-income neighborhoods where more community involvement and police discretion are common.

The United States Supreme Court has ruled that public school administrators may conduct reasonable searches of students without meeting the Constitutional standard of probable cause that applies to police. (26)

In 1986, President Ronald Reagan confirmed that he had directed a secret operation to be known as the "Iran-Contra affair." Several government officials were prosecuted for carrying out activities with the Nicaraguan Contras through secret private operatives. There were accusations that funds to purchase weapons to be traded to the government of Iran in exchange for the release of American hostages had been secured partially through narcotics smuggling into the United States from Central America.

EPILOGUE

Although the format of this book suggests that by correctly identifying true from false legal statements, a layperson may learn to unravel the intricacies of jurisprudence, the following reasons suggest that no one can ever achieve that ability completely.

❋ ❋ ❋

1. Since the law changes daily, concepts of the rules are only temporary.

2. Legal doctrines are different in every different jurisdiction. That is why the word "generally" is used so frequently in the chapters of this book.

3. All the rules of law have exceptions to them that must be understood.

4. The legal system is not really interested in "the truth." The system was only created to resolve disputes and settle disagreements among parties.

5. The rules of evidence frequently make "the truth" inadmissible in court.

6. Since the power to make laws rests with legislatures, when courts decide to make laws, they must disguise their legislating by using fictions.

In one New Jersey appellate court opinion, judges actually held that "statutes are not meant to be read literally."

7. Courts base the authority for their rulings on clauses that they find in the Constitution. Unfortunately, a literal reading of the Constitution is unable to disclose many of these important clauses. For example, where does the "right of privacy" appear?

8. Even the Supreme Court's authority to interpret the Constitution, called "judicial review," was actually a power that a Chief Justice created since article III of the Constitution makes no provision for courts to judge whether statutes comply with the court's interpretation of the Constitution.

Consequently, in legal practice, there are no firm answers, only suggestions of possible arguments that can be made on one side of an issue or another. Rather than memorization of legal rules and doctrines, mastering the law really depends upon having a creative and fertile imagination and the stamina to argue continuously in all directions until your purpose is achieved.

APPENDIX

The following portions of the first ten Amendments to the United States Constitution are relevant to the legal doctrines expressed in this book:

Amendment IV.

- the right of the people to be secure in their persons, houses, papers, and effects, against unreasonable searches and seizures shall not be violated.

- no warrants shall issue, but upon probable cause, supported by oath or affirmation.

- particularly describing the place to be searched, and the persons or things to be seized.

Amendment V.

- nor shall any person be subject for the same offense to be put twice in jeopardy of life or limb.

- nor shall be compelled in any criminal case to be a witness against himself.

- nor be deprived of life, liberty, or property, without due process of law.

- no person shall be held to answer for a capital, or otherwise infamous crime, unless on presentment or indictment of a grand jury.

Amendment VI.

- the accused shall enjoy the right to a speedy and public trial, by an impartial jury of the state and district wherein the crime shall have been committed.

- to be informed of the nature and cause of the accusation.

- to be confronted with the witnesses against him.

- to have compulsory process for obtaining witnesses in his favor.

- to have the assistance of counsel for his defense.

Amendment VII.

- the right of trial by jury shall be preserved.

- no fact tried by a jury, shall be otherwise re-examined in any court of the United States, than according to the rules of common law.

Amendment VIII.

- excessive bail shall not be required.

- nor excessive fines imposed.

- nor cruel and unusual punishments inflicted.

Amendment IX.

- the enumeration in the Constitution, of certain rights, shall not be construed to deny or disparage others retained by the people.

Amendment X.

- the powers not delegated to the United States by the Constitution, nor prohibited by it to the states, are reserved to the states respectively, or to the people.

Relevant case law:

1. Brown v. Board of Education of Topeka, Kansas, 1954

2. Plessy v. Ferguson, 1896

3. Marbury v. Madison, 1803

4. Griswold v. Connecticut, 1965

5. Roe V. Wade, 1973

6. Ozawa v. U.S., 1922

7. U.S. v. Thind, 1923

8. Miranda v. Arizona, 1966

9. Koon v. U.S., 1996

10. California v. Simpson, 1995

11. Furman v. Georgia, 1972, Greg v. Georgia, 1976

12. North Carolina v. Alford, 1968

13. U.S. v. Salerno, 1977

14. Illinois v. Perkins, 1990

15. Illinois v. Caballes, 2004

16. J.E.B. v. Alabama, 1994

17. California v. Greenwood, 1988

18. Oliver v. U.S., 1984

19. Horton v. California, 1990
20. Terry v. Ohio, 1968
21. U.S. v. Wade, 1967
22. Harris v. New York, 1971
23. Lawrence v. Texas, 2003
24. Illinois v. Leopold and Loeb, 1924
25. Massachusetts v. Sacco and Vanzetti, 1927
26. New Jersey v. T.L.O., 1984

ABOUT THE AUTHOR

Professor Giles Wayne Casaleggio

Giles Wayne Casaleggio is an associate professor of Criminal Justice at Saint John's University, College of Professional Studies. He obtained his Bachelor of Science Degree in Management from Fairleigh Dickinson University in 1972. He attended The University of Tennessee Law School and received his Juris Doctorate from Saint John's University in 1972. He was admitted to practice law in New York, New Jersey, and before The United States Supreme Court. He began his legal career in 1972 as a law clerk in the United States Attorney's Office for the Southern District of New York. From 1973 to 1985, He served as assistant prosecutor in Union County, New Jersey, and Chief Assistant Prosecutor in Passaic and Morris Counties, where he specialized in the investigation of organized crime and supervised their narcotics task forces. He received specialized training in electronic surveillance investigation at the Cornell University Institute on Organized Crime and was designated as an instructor for The New Jersey Police Training Commission. In 1985, He was appointed to the position of New Jersey Deputy Attorney General and assigned to investigate cases of political corruption and organized crime. He later co-authored the Attorney General's State Narcotics Action Plan and was designated as supervisor of Northern New Jersey operations of The State Police Narcotic Unit. In 1988, He entered local politics in New Jersey and was elected twice as mayor of his community.

BOOKS BY THIS AUTHOR

**Lore Enforcement:
The Need To... "Make American Justice Relate Again."**

In an effort to obtain research material for this book, I searched for a source that might provide a fresh perspective on the evolving effects of criminal justice services on various population groups within the United States. I considered interviewing individuals experiencing widely publicized negative interactions with policing agencies, such as members of the American underclass descended from conditions of involuntary servitude and those multilingual groups derived from foreign immigration or asylum seeking. Instead, however, I chose to express the reflections of a retired veteran of law enforcement whose ethnic identity is not often considered as that of an oppressed minority. Although they were the earliest of observers of the institution of European law and order in America, Native Americans are rarely popularized as the recipients of police injustices. Similarly, their contributions to American law enforcement are rarely acknowledged. Securing the valuable insights, criticisms, and recommendations of a qualified Amerindian law enforcement observer and practitioner, such as Captain Manitouabewich, has been enlightening and stimulating.

Magistrate In Mobster-Ville: The Strategies And Struggles Of A Prosecuting Attorney Battling Crime And Corruption In Cajun Country (Second Edition).

Magistrate in Mobster-Ville is a novel that takes place within the metropolitan area of New Orleans, Louisiana. It illustrates the life of a young lawyer who devotes his career to the investigation and prosecution of crimes while negotiating the roadblocks of governmental bureaucracy. While the characters, occurrences, and venues discussed in this novel are fictitious, American district attorney's offices routinely deal with the types of bizarre events depicted in its chapters. In reality, prosecutors are rarely celebrated for their legal successes, but their infrequent miscalculations are publicly scrutinized by appellate courts and media outlets. The prospective reader may tend to question the motivation of a young law school graduate in pursuing a career within this thankless profession. The target audience for this work might be those considering a career in law enforcement or litigation or those who are already veterans of one of these career paths. I believe that it outlines most of the possible avenues and deviations that such a career might lead one to travel.

Management Methods From The Mafia

"Management Methods From The Mafia" is intended to inspire creative leadership alternatives by recounting the techniques employed by 30 notorious mobsters of the past. Intended primarily for future law enforcement administrators, its concepts are also applicable to other organizational fields where innovative management procedures are long overdue. What better vehicle to carry the message of creative and efficient organizational management than the study of the successful entrepreneurs of infamous national crime syndicates?

"Management Methods From The Mafia" is an attempt to encourage exploration of these radical approaches to the organizational challenges facing government and industry in the twenty-first century. There may be three distinct types of readers that this book might appeal to: those interested in organizational management and leadership seeking new inspiration, those who find encouragement if the fact that something positive can be found even the deepest levels of evil in our society's history, and finally, those who are merely fascinated with the lives of the most notorious gangsters of the

Twentieth Century.

The strategies and philosophies that the author has assigned to each of the characters in this book are based upon the conclusions that he has have drawn from their biographies and accomplishments in real life. He has attempted to represent both genders and numerous ethnic groups his selection. Perhaps readers will draw differing conclusions and find inspiration in areas which he has not anticipated from reading about the experiences of these historical villains.

www.ingramcontent.com/pod-product-compliance
Lightning Source LLC
Chambersburg PA
CBHW020445220526
45464CB00002B/864